Social Media
Marketing Jump

Give Yourself A Head Start
In Social Media Marketing

SOCIAL MEDIA MARKETING JUMP
Give Yourself A Head Start In Social Media Marketing

© H.B.F. Editorial, 2014
© Charlie G. Fletcher
   Master Resell Rights

ISBN-13: 978-1500983284
ISBN-10: 1500983284

Table of Contents

Disclaimer

INTRODUCTION

WHAT IN THE WORLD IS SOCIAL MEDIA MARKETING

Any business that does not use social media marketing strategies these days is missing out on all the benefits that such strategies can bring your business. Just think of how far they've come from being considered as novelty about five years ago. Now, businesses and organizations simply cannot do without social media. In fact, it is already considered a critical part of their marketing mix.

In 2013, more marketers looked to social media marketing with more value. About 86% of them cited that social media is a significant part of their business, while 89% of them said that it benefits them by increasing their exposure to the market.

Social media marketing can give several benefits, such as increased exposure, improved traffic, more loyal fans, increased leads, new business relationships, improved search engine ranking, increased sales, reduced marketing costs, and better marketplace insight.

The fact that Facebook already has more than 1.26 billion users, with 1.23 billion of them being active on the social networking site every month, is more than enough proof of how big social media has become. And this is expected to continue in the years to come. Now, why would you choose to miss out all these benefits when you can start learning more about social media marketing right away?

CHAPTER 1

GROWING YOUR BUSINESS VIA SOCIAL MEDIA

You can develop your business using social media. But it all starts with being active on the social networks that matter and never let the customers forget about you. One way to continue reminding them that you're still around is to make some noise on your social pages.

As a business owner, you should at least have a basic working knowledge of what social media marketing is all about. You should know how to connect with people, especially your target market, through social media, to create excellent content that moves people to act, and to create relationships.

Social media marketing is about communicating with your target audience, informing them about your business, and eventually getting them involved. It could produce customer feedback, leads, and the opportunity to give them excellent customer service. But you will not get the response that you are hoping for unless you share your information the right way.

There are a few steps that you need to follow if you want to use social media to help your business grow.

DEVELOP A STRATEGIC PLAN

Social media marketing must be executed with a strategy that encompasses your goal and the measures of success. The best plan is to develop social media engagement. It should include how frequently you are going to produce content, what the voice of the business will be, and what response you expect to get from the people. It is not about hard selling, but about forging relationships. Do not overdo your sales pitch. Instead, try to gain your audience's trust.

STIR THE INTEREST OF YOUR POTENTIAL CUSTOMERS

Monitor and update your social media accounts regularly so as not to neglect the queries, comments and even complaints of your potential customers or existing ones. Timely responses are necessary to lower the chances of ruining customer relationships. It would be even better to attract your customers' attention using visuals, such as beautiful or funny photos, which are often easy to share. Hone your timing in joining conversations. You can also look for the latest object of your customers' affection by searching for #hashtags, Facebook posts, or tweets.

BUILD A SOCIAL MEDIA COMMUNITY FOR GREAT PROJECTS

Social media marketing can be used for the long haul. You can maximize its potentials if you get help from a social media community, such as Facebook, Twitter, or LinkedIn, who shares the same interests as you do. You can convince friends and their friends and colleagues to join that community, but as it grows, rules must be established.

BLOG, BLOG, BLOG

Blogging is a proven effective tool in social media marketing. Your blog serves as your home base with your Facebook, Twitter, and other social media sites serving as feeders that bring traffic to your blog. Every new blog brings new sales and traffic opportunities. The typical consumer behavior is to read about 10 blogs before making a buying decision.

ENGAGE THROUGH SOCIAL MEDIA

If you're on social media, be prepared to interact with followers. This means starting conversations, responding to questions, and being friends with your customers online. Use it to forge relationships.

AVOID HARD SELLING

Do not abuse the social media sites as your avenue for selling. Instead, focus more on engaging your followers instead of bombarding them with calls to action do something for you, if you don't want them to stop following you.

Whatever social media outlet becomes popular over the years, one thing is for sure – social media marketing will always be useful to businesses and marketers.

CHAPTER 2

SOCIAL MEDIA STATISTICS YOU SHOULD KNOW

If you want to make the most out of your social media account, it is important that you know how to use it and knowing the latest social media statistics would help.

Here are the latest statistics that you need to know before creating your social media strategies:

- **The most passionate advocates have the smallest following**. When social monitoring site Mention studied more than 1 billion social mentions for two years, they learned that 91% of mentions are made by people with less than 500 followers.

  While you should interact with power users, don't forget about engaging social media users with a few followers because most of them will be the ones talking about you.

  - **Written content is more valuable than visuals, according to marketers**. A 3,000-respondent survey by Social Media Examiners among marketers showed that about 58% of them believe that original written content is the most important form of content in social media, while only 19% valued visuals.

  Use written content to establish yourself as an expert in your niche and improve brand awareness. Post a good story about your brand.

  - **Retweets are best done late at night**. They are most effective when done between 10pm and 11pm ET and on Sundays, according to Track Maven. They should also come with the world "Retweet" in all caps or with exclamation points to increase retweets.

  You can test this theory out and see how it impacts your engagement.

  - **Twitter responses have to be done in less than an hour**. According to a Lithium Technologies research, 53% of the users who tweet you expect your reply within the hour.

Use tools to monitor your customer support tweets and check your Twitter email alerts to respond to your tweets fast.

- **Fridays are the best day of the week for Facebook users.** According to Adobe, Fridays receive more likes, shares, and comments than any other day of the week, after analyzing more than 225 billion Facebook posts.

Make sure to include Friday for your Facebook posting schedule.

- **Twitter, Facebook and Pinterest are the most effective traffic drivers.** Social sharing website Shareaholic showed that that these three social media sites that refer more traffic. On the other hand, Google+, LinkedIn, and YouTube are the top three sites when it comes to pages per visit, time on site, and bounce rate.

If you want to increase brand awareness, choose Twitter and Facebook, and maybe Pinterest, too. If you're aiming for qualified traffic, focus more on YouTube, Google+ and LinkedIn.

- **Pinterest has a different category pulling in the most engagement each day.** Monday is for fitness; Tuesday is for technology; Wednesday is for inspirational quotes; Thursday is for fashion; Friday is for humor; Saturday is for travel; and Sunday is for food and crafts.

Make a Pinterest board that covers all these topics and create a schedule based on the findings above.

- **Target 28, 118, or 385 interactions for each Facebook post.** According to Social Bakers, social media pages with up to 9,999 fans need 28 interactions per post; those with 10,000 to 99,999 fans need 118; and those with 100,000 to 499,999 fans need 385.

Interactions refer to shares, comments, and likes in total. The more interactions your post gets, the wider its reach.

Monitor your Facebook page using these benchmarks.

- **There are 6 unique conversation networks on Twitter.** These are the following:

a. Polarized crowds, which discuss polarizing topics, such as politics, and do not interact with groups they are in disagreement with;

b. Tight crowds, which usually consist of professionals, conferences, or hobby groups that interact about ideas, opinions, and information;

c. Brand clusters, which discuss celebrities and products that are of mass interest but with minimal connectivity;

d. Community clusters, which discuss popular topics and global news events and are often disconnected from each other;

e. Broadcast network, which usually consists of the loyal followers of pundits and media outlets who have little interaction with each other;

f. Support network, which are created as government agencies, organizations, and companies respond to customer queries, requests, and complaints, with the company or organization replying to disconnected users.

If you want brand engagement, target the community clusters and tight crowds, and possibly the support networks. Find the Twitter network that suits you best.

CHAPTER 3

SOCIAL MEDIA PLATFORMS THAT REALLY MATTER

Social media is here to stay, that is, if you want to maintain your online existence. Marketers hold onto it for their business' dear life. But if you use it for the sole purpose of marketing, this is when things might get confusing.

HOW TO CHOOSE A PLATFORM

That's because there are a lot of social media sites, various methods to engage your audience, and the different styles used in each platform. So how you should you choose the best platform for you? You will find out after answering these questions.

- **What does your target audience use?**

Determine which social media site your audience use. Not all your followers are actual people.

- **Which site has the most active audience?**

Having many users does not automatically mean lots of activity. Google has 1 billion users, but only 35% were actively using their account in the past month.

- **Which site does your audience use for searching?**

Every minute, millions of searches are done on Google, Facebook and Twitter. If you stay active on these platforms, your audience may find you.

- Which is the most suitable social media site for your niche?

If one site works for others, it might not necessarily work for you because of your niche. Find one that is frequented by businesses with the same offering as you have.

Use these questions to guide you to which platform you should use.

THE TOP FOUR SOCIAL MEDIA PLATFORMS

The top four sites that really matter include Facebook, Twitter, LinkedIn, and Google+.

Facebook

Facebook is the biggest social network with its more than 1.3 billion users. It has been around for 10 years, with more than half of its users actively using it daily. Each visit lasts for 18 minutes on average.

Aside from browsing for updates or looking at photos, a Facebook is also connected to about 80 pages, events or groups. This is how you can reach them.

Twitter

Each Twitter user, who has an average of 208 followers and 307 Tweets and spends an average of 170 minutes on their profile, presents a marketing opportunity. Half of its signups remain active daily, with 29% of them visiting their Twitter several times each day.

Twitter is more about engaging customers for their brand loyalty. About 85% of Twitter users feel a connection to a business that they are following on Twitter.

LinkedIn

There are two new LinkedIn sign ups every second. Now, it has over 270 million users, creating another social media giant.

Marketers love Facebook, Twitter, and Google+ and often ignore LinkedIn. However, LinkedIn is actually the ideal platform for B2B marketing.

The site is proud of its mostly professional users, who are linked to companies. If you don't want to miss out on a lot of social media love, make sure to stay active on LinkedIn, too.

Google+

Marketers consider 2014 as Google+'s year. They even predicted its growing impact on social media, which did come true.

Given how Google+ is backed up by the biggest search engine in the world and the effect of Google Authorship, it's no surprise that it has become as big as it is today. It is now an engagement mine due to its collaboration with Hangouts.

Whatever it is that you are trying to sell, say or do for the sake of marketing, make sure to stay active on these social media platforms.

CHAPTER 4

HOW SOCIAL MEDIA TRAFFIC CAN BOOST YOUR WEBSITE RANKING

There are claims that search engines are out and social media is in when it comes to searching for information online. However, this is not the case now, but there might be merit to such claims. Social media has truly changed the way people find and share content, although it has not totally removed the significance of Google, Bing and Yahoo to searchers.

But one thing that is certain is that social media has become an important factor that search engines consider when indexing content. It affects your website ranking in various ways.

SOCIAL SHARES ARE CONSIDERED LINK BUILDING

For years, businesses have used both legitimate and illegitimate ways to get links to their website and improve their rankings. However, things have changed.

Now, links are obtained by creating original content and sharing it online, especially across social media. Links from your Facebook, LinkedIn, Google+, Twitter, YouTube, and other social networks to your content will show the search engines that your website is credible with useful content and that it should be ranked for the keyword phrases that you used.

Look at how a link that is retweeted a number of times compared to a link that did not receive a single tweet will be more visible in Google and other search engines since it is assumed to have more valuable content for being shared several times on social media.

Produce great content on social media to attract audiences and search engines alike. But the most important thing is still to engage your followers and establish real relationships with them to gain their trust and hopefully, their social shares.

SOCIAL MEDIA CONTENT SPEEDS UP INDEXATION PROCESS

Search engines consider content shared across social networks. The more links your website gets, the quicker it gets indexed. Since social media can drive links to your web content faster, it can usually hasten the indexation process.

For instance, content that has received more retweets may cut indexation time by 50, while cutting the time it takes for the search engine bots to locate your content from two hours to two seconds.

SOCIAL MEDIA MARKETING INCREASES BRAND AWARENESS

When you talk to people on Facebook, Twitter, or any other social network, you seem more "real" to them. Your image is now more than just a corporation that is disconnected from your customers. Instead, you talk to them while tackling real issues related to your products and services. It is like having an actual relationship with them, which will likely give you customer loyalty and long-term business.

VALUABLE CONTENT ON SOCIAL MEDIA IS SHAREABLE

If people find useful or informative content on social media, they would share it with friends and followers to spread the information or make their profile more interesting. But regardless of the reason why they share it, the most important thing is that they are helping spread the word about your business. The wider the reach of the information, the better it will be for your website rankings.

KEYWORDS FROM YOUR SOCIAL MEDIA PROFILE AND CONTENT BOOST YOUR KEYWORD RANKING

They keywords found on your social media account and the content posted in it will have an impact on your content ranking in search engines. Usually, search engines look at your URL, name, and bio. That's why you need to fill your profile with relevant information while naturally inserting the name of your company and your keywords.

These are only some of the ways social media affect your website rankings. But the bottom line will always be that it has become an even bigger factor for search engines to consider while determining website rankings.

CHAPTER 5

INCREASING YOUR BLOG TRAFFIC WITH SOCIAL MEDIA MARKETING

Seeing as how influential social media marketing can be to the promotion of your business, you need to find ways to maximize its benefits, especially in driving traffic to your website. You may even focus on increasing your blog traffic using several techniques that involve the social networks.

Here are some ways to drive traffic to your blog using social media marketing:

- Publish blog content on your social media. There are tools that will automatically post links to your blog content on your Facebook or Twitter profiles. Link it to your Google+, LinkedIn, and other social media accounts as well. Familiarize yourself with the different social media profile settings so you'll know how to take care of issues such as this.

- Link your social media profile to your blog. Include the URL of your blog in your social media profiles. It should be found in your Facebook profile, Twitter bio, LinkedIn profile, and YouTube channel description, among others.

- Put 'follow me' on your blogs. Add the 'follow me' icon to your blog's sidebar to encourage people to connect with you via Facebook, Twitter, Google+, and other social networks. Even if people did not initially visit your blog, they would have a way to easily find it through your social media profile.

- Simplify social media sharing for your visitors. Your blog should be easy to share on your readers' social media profiles. Put visually noticeable social sharing icons on your blog's sidebar or home page, or at the bottom of each post.

- Take advantage of social tools and widgets. Social media sites usually have free tools and widgets to help promote your blog content and increase its exposure on your profile. Add them to your blog or websites.

- Promote blog contests on your social media profiles. These should help drive short-term traffic to your blog, while increasing awareness about the contest.

- Use cross-profile publishing tools. There are scheduling tools like TweetDeck, SproutSocial, or HootSuite that can automatically publish the links to your blog content on several social media profiles simultaneously. This should be less hassle on your part.

- Join social media groups and share your relevant content. You can find many of these groups on LinkedIn and Facebook. Search for active groups on these social media platforms that discuss topics relevant to yours. Join them and interact with the other members by posting comments and starting conversations. Eventually, you might get to share the links to your most relevant blog content without being too promotional about it.

- Stay active on social media. Aside from publishing your blog posts on your social media profiles, be active and interact with other users. Retweet their tweets and share their content too.

- Gather people on social media. You could try a TweetChat and talk about your topic or any other relevant topic. Make your relationships real by meeting your local followers and fellow tweeters.

- Change your existing content to suit various social media destinations. You could convert YouTube videos into tweets, SlideShare presentations, blog posts, podcasts or any other form of social media content. This should increase exposure for that specific content on social media.

CHAPTER 6

HOW TO INCREASE YOUR SOCIAL MEDIA CLICKTHROUGH RATES

To effectively drive traffic to your website via social media, you have to improve your social media clickthrough rates first.

Remember that your website is where your target audience will find answers to their questions and where they can start a potential relationship with you as your readers. It is also where you can give them value and even encourage them to buy from you.

However, you can't assume that all your social followers and fans will go to your website. You need to give them a little more encouragement to proceed to your website and start establishing a relationship with them. You can do that following these steps.

GIVE YOUR FOLLOWERS A CLEAR CALL-TO-ACTION

Tell them what to do, which is to visit your website.

No matter how great and shareable your posts and images are, they would remain useless without any effect on your clickthrough rate if they don't include a link to your blog or website. Aside from the link, you can also establish branding by including your logo or company name in your posts.

Once your posts with your branding and link are shared, this will increase exposure for your website and possibly increase your clickthrough rates as well.

Don't commit the common mistake of not telling your fans what you need them to do. Be clear in telling them that you want them to join a membership, to buy what you are selling, or to follow them on your other social media accounts, then give them a link to help them complete their action.

GIVE YOUR FOLLOWERS ENOUGH MOTIVATION TO CLICK THROUGH

Don't waste your content by missing out on an opportunity to engage your followers and fans. Make sure each post or tweet is smart, shareable, and informative to get your audience's attention. It would be even better if your updates are about a solution to the issues that many of the people in your audience are dealing with because such updates tend to get more shares, comments, or likes.

Although you can talk about how great your products and services are, it is even more powerful if someone trustworthy and respected talk about. This is when you usually see how influential social media is. Your followers tend to click through to your website when an influential figure suggests they should check out something.

You may also give them a deadline to spur them into action, the same principle used in limited time offers.

MAKE A COHESIVE UPDATE

When you post updates on your social media profile, make sure to keep them consistent and cohesive. The title should fit the text, the image, and the call to action.

Treat previous updates that obtained a good response from your audience as your benchmark. Write an update with the same message to get the same response and eventually increase your clickthrough rate.

EXCITE FANS WITH YOUR LANDING PAGE

You owe it to them to give them an interesting landing page. Excite them about doing what you want them to do.

For instance, if you want to get their email address and give them a free article in return, lead them to a landing page that will give them more information about what you expect them to do, reinforce it with another clear call to action, and tell them how to complete that action.

If you want more conversions, forge strong relationships with your fans. Give them more value and expect them to click through.

CHAPTER 7:

EVERYTHING YOU NEED TO KNOW ABOUT SOCIAL ENGAGEMENT

What is social engagement?

While you may be busy posting updates on Facebook, Twitter, Google+ or any of your social media profiles, you are merely considered to be performing a social activity. This refers to any event within a social media platform that involves you directly or indirectly.

Events that do not impact you directly do not need your immediate attention. But those that involve you, such as getting a new follower, comment, or share is what you call social engagement and this is what you need.

Social engagement is an event on your social media profile that has a direct effect on your social existence. Examples would be new comments, shares, retweets, check-ins, likes, views, or click-throughs, among others.

The more engagement you get, the better, because this could lead to new fans and followers who will likely do what you want them to do. You could get them to subscribe to your blog or even to purchase something from you. This is because these are usually people who are interested in what you have to offer and who usually need a little push to become a customer.

But it does not end there. Once these followers do something for you, you have to do something for them too! You could respond to their comment or talk to them. Treat them as though they are your friends, even if there are hundreds or thousands of them!

To get this social engagement going, you need to establish an action plan that includes a series of activities that you need to do once you engage a follower. This is what you call as social strategy.

So, how can you encourage more social engagement?

SHOWCASE YOUR EMPLOYEES AND EVENTS TO YOUR FOLLOWERS

Hardworking employees are the heart of every great company.

SEOMoz, for instance, started a Facebook photo album showing pictures of their employees, making it even more interesting with a "Then and Now" theme.

If you also have company events, you can start a Facebook Event so your followers can take note of it and include it in their calendar. It could be webinars, seminars, charity events, conferences, or open houses. This will make your followers feel as though they are part of your community.

CONVERT CUSTOMERS INTO BRAND ADVOCATES

This is the latest trend in social media marketing. If someone tweets positively or post a video about your company, repost it! It conveys a more authentic message to your audience. Find ways to encourage people to talk about you or your band.

REWARD FANS

As your loyal audience, your fans deserve to be rewarded. It could be a gift card, a T-shirt, or a product showcasing your brand. Watch how your interactions will grow, not to mention the Twitter handles, email addresses, and phone numbers that you can collect for future marketing campaigns.

BE MOBILE FRIENDLY

Keep your messages and updates short, given the short attention span of the users these days. They tend to read shorter posts than long paragraphs. The shorter the better!

USE THE RIGHT TONE

It all depends on your target audience. If you are dealing with customers, it might be best to sound casual. But you should also consider your product or service. For instance, a luxury brand might sound more appealing if they sound more formal when engaging their audience.

If you are dealing with businesses, it's best to sound formal, but not stuffy and uptight. Even if you have CEOs and industry figures as your followers, it doesn't mean you can't have fun with your social media content.

CHAPTER 8

TRACKING SOCIAL MEDIA TRAFFIC

Monitoring social media traffic is an important part of social media marketing. This is how you will know if your tactics are working and what you should do to improve which area. It is a good thing that there are tools that you can use to track social media traffic.

GOOGLE ANALYTICS AND SOCIAL MEDIA METRICS PLUGIN

Google Analytics is likely the most popular monitoring tool in the market because of its comprehensive analytics. It can monitor all your traffic sources, although it does not only focus on social networks. If you want a more in-depth look at your social media traffic alone, use a complementary monitoring tool, such as the Social Media Metrics plugin. It will show your social metrics and traffic based on Google Analytics. You can see the most valuable metrics, from page views to page's activity on your social media account.

SOCIAL METRICS PLUGIN FOR WORDPRESS

This free WordPress plugin monitors your blog's performance on all major social networking. Despite the limited information, it gives useful and direct- to-the-point metrics. Social Metrics monitor each of your blog posts and gather how many shares each one has on the major social media platforms. This shows which blog posts received the most response, hence determining what your followers are interested in and what you should write about in your next blog posts.

FACEBOOK INSIGHTS

This tool from Facebook will show who likes your posts and page, how many people visited your page, what type of content are the most popular, and other useful statistics. Even if it does not give you the exact social media traffic, it determines which content your Facebook fans love to read. Use it to optimize your Facebook content and drive more traffic to your site.

VIRALHEAT

This tool may cost you around $50, but it can monitor 15 social accounts and two search profiles on Facebook, Twitter, Pinterest, the web, and video.

You can use it to compare relevant terms and profiles across social media accounts and the web so you can monitor individual products and their buzz and compare them to your other products or the products of your competitors.

Viralheat can determine if your social media efforts have improved buzz about your brand on the web.

SOCIAL MENTION

This is one of the most user-friendly monitoring tools that you can use, since you only need to search for your company name or keyword and get interesting insights such as strength, reach, sentiment, average per mentions, top users using the same keywords, and other figures. This can determine which topics created the strongest buzz on social media, so you will know what you should tweet or post about to increase engagement.

TWEETREACH

This is another simple social monitoring tool that can show you the reach of your tweets. Connect it to your Twitter account and search for anything, from a URL to a hashtag or a Twitter screen name.

TweetReach will then show you the top contributors and their contribution, the number of accounts that were reached, the most popular retweets, and a timeline. This can determine how popular your tweets are, who contributed the most, and who your influencers are.

Although you need to monitor your website traffic, don't neglect your social traffic if you want to use it as a platform to promote your business. To get the best results, monitor it as well using the tools mentioned above and more.

CHAPTER 9

MEASURING YOUR SOCIAL MEDIA SUCCESS

While many companies are busy launching social media campaigns after realizing its value to their marketing mix, not many of them have perfected the idea of measuring their success with social media. It goes beyond the number of followers or likes, because as per studies, more than 80% of these "likers" never visit the page again.

So how do you know if you are successful or not? These three measures will help you answer that question.

REACH

This measures how many people you have influenced with your message. It shows just how much your target audience likes your content.

Some Reach metrics include the following:

- Twitter followers

- LinkedIn connections

- Facebook page likers

- Blog visitors

- YouTube viewers and subscribers.

Use analytics reports from the social networks to monitor these metrics. You can also use third-party social monitoring tools to keep track of your Reach.

ENGAGEMENT

This refers to how many people you have interacted with. Once you have identified how many people have seen your message, it's time to see how many of them cared enough to act on it. To interact with people on social media, you need to spur them into action using valuable content. Low engagement levels mean that you have to change your content for something better.

Some Engagement metrics include the following:

- Retweets, direct messages, and mentions on Twitter

- Click-throughs in your posts

- Comments and shares on your LinkedIn and Facebook posts

- Comments on your blog content

- Ratings on YouTube videos

You can also use third-party services to measure your social media engagement.

CONVERSION

This refers to how many people acted based on your call to action. Conversion determines the impact that your social media marketing efforts make on your business. It shows how many of your followers and fans on social media took the next step, as per your call to action, to become new leads and a part of your marketing database. It is important to use your company website as the hub to which all your social media content are linked to. All your Facebook posts, Twitter tweets, or LinkedIn posts should link back to your website content. It also helps to include lead generation offers and upsells on your website to identify your anonymous traffic and convert them into named leads.

Some Conversion metrics include the following:

- Webinar sign ups

- Content download registrations

- Online sales

- Leads from phone calls

- Completed online forms

There are several free monitoring tools that you can use, such as Google Analytics, which can monitor the activities in your website. You can also incorporate trackable links for every social media post. Don't miss out on the goal tracking feature of Google Analytics too, to monitor your conversion activities. This will complete your social monitoring tools to keep track of your social media success.

CHAPTER 10

THE FUTURE OF SOCIAL MEDIA

As more marketers are using social media to promote their products and services, what do you think this marketing platform has left to offer in the future?

SOCIAL MEDIA IS MATURING

When social media was first introduced, it created such a splash among early adopters. Now, it is an important part of an individual user's and a marketer's life. However, that importance goes beyond the fact that it is something new, but rather because it has proven its worth. This is how social media has matured and grown in value to the marketing world and to society in general.

Social media has undergone a few significant changes. While it used to be a platform for anything viral, it has now become a platform for meaningful engagement. Now, companies need to ensure that they not only have a Facebook account, but that they are also active in it while engaging their followers by posting informative, relevant content.

Consumers now use social media to engage with their favorite brands. They use it to relay their message to the companies and to fellow consumers.

SOCIAL MEDIA MAKES DATA EVEN MORE VALUABLE

It is expected that companies will be keener on connecting with their customers to turn them into loyal buyers. To do that, they need to use proximity data, purchase history, search history, and social media posts, among others, to create a message that will push a potential customer to go to the store or to click through to the website without bothering that customer.

The root concept here is "connection." By combining customer information with the impact of social media, you can create a more personal interaction with prospects in real time.

You can resolve customer complaints or answer customer queries faster because of all the information that you can get your hands on via customer relationship management. Soon enough, it may be possible for you to walk by your favorite local restaurant and get a tweet about an offer on their specials.

MARKETING PROGRAMS WILL IMPROVE

Social media will become a more central component to content-based marketing programs.

Brands will become mobile-friendly because of how most consumers will rely on their mobile devices to access the web and search for products and services. But the change lies in the customers' expectations of what social media can do for them.

Social media will be used more than just a tool to communicate and promote your offers to the customers. It will become an effective tool to engage and create loyal customers out of your social media followers and fans. This makes social marketing the heart of your marketing plan, not just an afterthought. Instead of hard selling, try talking to your customers through social media and find out what they need, what they really think of your offers, and what they expect from your brand.

IT'S ALL GOING MOBILE

Mobile is going to dominate over desktop when it comes to accessing the Internet. In fact, it's starting to show now. But it is more than just using tablets and smartphones connected to cars. Your car dashboard will have a built-in touchscreen browser, a technology that you can now find in Tesla Model S, the first of its kind of vehicular mobile Internet.

Then there's wearable technology, such as Google Glass, that revolutionizes connectivity. Google has just announced adding more sales channels for their wearable product, which might soon enough before major eyewear brands will also get their hands on this technology.

As a result, you need to make your content and social media platforms mobile-friendly. This means creating shorter text content, introducing tappable elements, and using video to improve mobile user experience. Try to include more visual elements to the mix.

CONTENT MARKETING WILL DEVELOP FURTHER

Content marketing is important as it is as a tool used by marketers to reach customers and improve website rankings. But the ability to create and post content used to be a problem among marketers.

Technology has helped deal with this challenge by introducing sleeker, cheaper, and user-friendly content management systems. CMS has made it easier to publish social content to promote their brands.

You can expect better technologies to possibly automate content creation.

While expecting these possible changes to social media, make sure that you are prepared to adapt to the trend. Get ahead of your competitors by allocating more budget to both social and mobile marketing strategies today. This will help you hone the necessary skills and ability to find effective social programs. You should try to perfect your monitoring, reviewing, and implementation processes for your social marketing efforts, too.

Marketers now expect social marketing to be the central component of their marketing efforts.

www.ingramcontent.com/pod-product-compliance
Lightning Source LLC
Chambersburg PA
CBHW060937050326
40689CB00013B/3134